# JUST BECAUSE HE IS...

By Linda Sheridan

Just Because He Is…

By Linda Sheridan

Cover Art Created: Isaac Brown III

Cover Concept: LeRoy Grayson

Logo Design: Justin Ackerman and Angel Jones

Editor: Craig Kavanaugh

Compiler: Anelda Attaway

© 2024 Linda Sheridan

ISBN 978-1-954425-96-5

Library of Congress Control Number: 2024904829

# DEDICATIONS

This book is dedicated to professed Christian women who are evaluating or dating professed Christian men. Those described in the Profile Section of this book represent sincere and genuine Christian men who behave as honestly as they know how; men who are not trying to deceive women, nor are they consciously aware that they do not make "healthy marriage or life partners." Again, no disparagement intended whatsoever; we are all flawed. The purpose of the book is to caution and dissuade women from accepting the false belief that their perceived "one" great asset will alone be the foundation of a healthy and fulfilling relationship.

# ACKNOWLEDGMENTS

First I thank God for the inspiration and good health to write this book. The writing began in 2020. I thank my early readers of the manuscript in its infancy. They are Elizabeth Conley, Kelly Ferraro, Hillary Givhan, Karen McCottry, and Faith & Gregg Mattison who gave me invaluable feedback. As I incorporated helpful suggestions, other friends Karen Raymond, Ann Schneider-Meisel, Deborah Thomas, Lynn Davis, and the late Deborah Johnson all encouraged me to journey on. During my hunt for publishers, Jackie Caine, Marsha Collick, Linda Montgomery, and Denise Hollingsworth provided information.

I thank Sheri Trueblood for referring me to Franklin Morris II, who tirelessly oriented me to the publishing world. I thank Carolyn Markland for referring me to Jazzy Kitty Publications, who extended merciful patience with me.

Life goes on whether or not one is writing a book. Outside of Christ and my biological and church families here are some of my life supporters: The Tuesday Evening Sisterhood; The Read Between the Lines Book Club; The 12 PM and 9 PM Prayer Groups; My walking partners Sharon Bryant and Brittany Richardson, and of course my road partners Lisa Lothian, Adrienne Grier, and Kimberly Harris.

# TABLE OF CONTENTS

Throughout this book, the reader will see the word bonding or its various synonyms mentioned quite a few times. Bonding has very broad implications and I would like to share what relationship authors have written about this crucial "cornerstone" of marriage.

**Quotes from:**

## The Sacred Marriage, What If God Designed Us To Make Us Holy More Than to Make Us Happy? By Gary Thomas

*"I think marriage is designed to call us out of ourselves and learn to love the "different."  Page 50*

*"As long as we are not mean, vindictive, or cruel we may think we're fulfilling the Christian duty. But we are not!" Page 161*

*"Love is an intentional movement toward another." Page 235*

*"Marriage calls us out of ourselves to help us remember that ours is not the only vision in the world." Page 261*

# THE FIRST TWO YEARS of MARRIAGE
## By Thomas N. Hart & Kathleen Fischer Hart

*"Marriage is defined by a positive virtue. It presumes the gift of self. ...One can do many external deeds of love and still hold back the really precious gift of the inner self."* Page 19

*"Marriage is a long walk a couple takes together... The travelers do not know where they are going nor when they will arrive."* Page 159

# AS FOR ME AND MY HOUSE by Walter Wangerin, Jr.

*"Remember three beings live within the construct of the marriage: the wife, a husband, and the relationship between them. When all the wife does and all the husband does are done to serve the third being, the relationship, when each detail of their toiling is a service to that, then they are sharing."* Page 138

*"Marriages have broken on the not sharing. Survival work must be the single job of both partners for the support of this single relationship."* Page 141

*"If anyone should establish for him/herself a life independent from his/her spouse, one which does not serve the marriage or which he/she tends to keep hidden from him/her, he/she has broken faith. He/She is not "sharing the work of survival."* Page 148

# LIES AT THE ALTAR by Robin Smith

*"If you are not marrying the soul of your partner you will not have anything to hold you together when the facade becomes unappealing"* Page 11

*"The first marriage vow should be "I promise to show up as a grown-up."* Page 26

*"A healthy relationship stretches us into growing the areas that are emotionally, spiritually and physically underdeveloped"* Page 58

*"There are too many people divorced today because they were unable to join their spouses in the present and engage fully in the task of building the future."* Page 66

*"What sets marriage apart from other close relationships is the total exposure... No other relationship approaches this level of exposure or vulnerability... [It] involves a commitment to the real process of being known and knowing the other...[It] means remaining available to your partner, staying in the present, and*

*closing the exits that serve as escape valves from the marriage relationship." Page 86*

*"Marriage is not a journey of aloneness. Its purpose is to create an environment where both individuals can be their true selves within the sacred bonds of the commitment." Page 105*

# INTRODUCTION

This book addresses heterosexual relationships who are Christian. The premise of the book centers around the ability to bond as being critical to a healthy marriage. The author maintains an assumption that most people naturally covet a certain special characteristic in a potential mate and are very often greatly influenced in their relationship decision-making by this particular characteristic that they find so charming or desirable. We are often tempted to make this "special asset" synonymous with "his ability to bond" in a lifetime partnership, but such is not necessarily the case. The author hopes to encourage women to not allow that coveted characteristic to become the dominant drawing card when pursuing or being pursued by a man.

It should be noted that the counsel to avoid allowing a single highly sought-after attribute or set of attributes to cloud our relational judgment in no way undermines the value of such attributes. The counsel simply means that we need to recognize that just possessing such attributes does not automatically make one able to bond in holy matrimony. Indeed, the twelve profiles that I will explore in the book are not to disparage any man; rather, the reader will discover that these attributes in and of themselves are laudable.

I would make two other introductory points:

(1) This book is neither a "witch hunt" to disparage men, nor a comprehensive guide to healthy relationships, and so I hope no one seeks to use it as the final screening tool for assessing the long-term viability of a relationship.

(2) Just because a woman is "eyeing" a man does not mean that she is viewing him with the healthiest eyes or mindset. Her view of the situation may be skewed by her own background or issues, in which she could be misreading or misinterpreting the behavior of a potential mate or suitor.

# CHAPTER 1

## A GOOD PROVIDER

**Profile**: He has a great job with good benefits, substantial current assets and retirement savings, and skills to continue to be a good and resourceful income earner. He is not in debt and manages money very well.

**Contemplation**: Being a reliable provider is a wonderful asset that makes women feel secure financially. In fact, this attribute may be especially admirable among women who may have had financially irresponsible dads. We all know that poor money management can cause debt, and unmanageable debt typically represents the "top reason" why people divorce. One might be tempted to think that Mr. Provider may make a good life partner because at least his good money management skills will give you a solid foundation as a couple to hopefully avoid that "top reason" for breaking up.

**Reality**: A good provider may in truth mean that you will not have to worry about money issues, but that does not mean that he will be as equally diligent regarding other matters that help make relationships work (e.g., emotional support, loving affection, shared recreational pursuits, etc.). Here are some potential concerns to consider: First, some men provide only as long as it unconsciously benefits himself (e.g., a nice house, car, pool, status, etc.). Second, being a good money manager may lead a man to want to benignly control all the household income, which may be difficult for an independent-minded woman to accept, especially one who has sound ideas as to how the money ought to be spent. Third, his earning a good salary may be the result of his being a workaholic, leaving little time for his wife and family, or may be the result of his loving his career or his status more than you, leading to him seeking promotions and/or other personal achievements over a harmonious home life. His frequent absence may negatively impact the marriage. Fourth, he may be a good provider out of a sense of duty and not out of the commitment of true love. Some men have been raised to believe that a husband's sole role is to provide, even at the expense of emotional support, loving affection, or bonding.

# CHAPTER 2

## A NICE PERSON

**Profile**: From what you can see and what others have said, he is a nice person. He is easygoing, courteous, affable, mind-mannered, helpful, blends well with all kinds of people, has an infectious laugh, and appears to have a level-headedness about him.

**Contemplation**: Surely, every Christian woman desires a truly nice and courteous man, whom others universally recognize for his kindness. Our hearts are often aglow in the presence of a man with a pleasant and engaging personality. One can be tempted to think that his niceness will certainly be a major asset in a lifetime arrangement.

**Reality**: First, what we see on the outside may be misleading. Just because he is truly nice to other people, and especially to you, during courtship, does not mean the niceness carries over to tough times. When there is no real "stake" involved, it can be relatively easy to appear nice. Being nice to someone you desire to know better is easy, but what about when involving the real commitment of being engaged and married? When real difficulties of life arise unexpectedly, will he still be nice then? Without commitment, there is no vulnerability. In a marriage, both parties need to be vulnerable and supportive, even amidst hurts, rejection, misunderstandings, etc. Second, some nice guys may fear making commitments, preferring rather to continue a boyfriend/girlfriend relationship indefinitely, especially when emotional and physical intimacy are shared too soon prior to commitment. Third, his niceness may be masking the fact that he is a "people pleaser." People pleasers who do not know how to say "no," nor know how to set firm boundaries, create a major problem for a potential lifetime partner.

# CHAPTER 3

## GREAT WITH CHILDREN AND/OR THE ELDERLY

**Profile**: You and others see that he has a nice way with children of all ages. He can make a sad child laugh or smile. He can help two middle schoolers stop fighting and work out their differences. He can calm down a rebellious teenager by speaking their language. He simply has the gift of working well with children. Or perhaps he is the "sweetheart" of the elderly, easily connecting with them, and always respectful and ready to help them with genuine care that is admirable.

**Contemplation**: When you see this man in action, you might think, "What a great asset that he has such meaningful interaction with children and/or the elderly." You greatly admire his people skills with these two groups. You might be tempted to think, "Gosh, he must be a good person to get along well with this population," harboring ideations about how he might be a great dad to your children, or your kids from a previous marriage, or to your parents who live with you now or may in the future.

**Reality**: Connecting with minors requires very different relational skills than connecting with adults. Why? The hierarchy is different; adults are equals. Some adults relate better to children because they feel there is no competition. Some men are fine with a basic conversation with their peers of the opposite sex but find themselves completely out of their league if forced to discuss any topic of serious substance or a complicated nature. Should children give him pushback, he copes satisfactorily because he can make an effort to work things out with them. If, however, an adult for whom he has feelings gives him pushback, he may not be able to transfer those same skills to working out an adult conflict. Instead, he may simply shut down; shutting down can tear a relationship apart.

# CHAPTER 4

## ONE WHO HAS AN ADMIRABLE MINISTRY
## IN THE COMMUNITY

**Profile**: He is very community service-minded, being committed to Christ's commandment that we serve others. He may dutifully perform one or many of the following outreach efforts: feeding the homeless, collecting needed items, counseling addicts, conducting seminars, volunteering at a shelter or food pantry, mentoring boys, visiting the sick and shut-in, driving the church van to pick up worshippers, helping citizens complete applications for services, rescuing dogs, organizing block cleanup projects, etc.

**Contemplation**: Christian women rightly admire seeing a Christian man who is serious about outreach to the community. You believe his focus on community service shows he cares for those less fortunate and that he willingly makes a sacrifice to help others as Christ has urged us to do. You attribute his behavior to kindness, nobility, generosity of spirit, selflessness, and Christlikeness. You are tempted to become convinced that he has the compassionate heart needed in a healthy marriage.

**Reality**: First, AMEN! He may sincerely possess all of these noble Christian attributes; indeed, we need more men who are serious about community outreach. Yet, do not assume that the heart he shows for the less fortunate will always be the same heart he shows for you. Not to suggest that he will intentionally hurt you, but rather it is possible that he may not have the same verve or passion for you as he has for serving God and others. Remember without vulnerability, the experiential opportunity for hurt, rejection, or pain is limited. Second, for some men, their commitment for outreach may take precedence over their presence in your marriage relationship (e.g., the founder of AA was so committed to helping others that he neglected his wife's needs until she left him; when he realized the cost of losing her, he finally purposed to get his wife back).

# CHAPTER 5

## CHARMING, IMPECCABLY COURTEOUS, CHIVALROUS, ROMANTIC, DEBONAIR, GENTLEMANLY, "OLD SCHOOL," POLITE AND RESPECTFUL OF WOMEN

**Profile**: This man accompanies his nice personality with an alluring charm. He may even have an accent to boost that charm (French, Italian, British, etc.) or even a deep bass voice. His parents taught him superb manners, diplomacy, and how to treat women with "kit gloves." He will not let a woman open a door, carry anything over two pounds, or sit down without pulling out her chair. If you are with him, he stands up when you enter or exit a room. He will not commence eating until you start. He calls unfamiliar women Madame. He tips his hat when he meets a woman for the first time. He places his hand gently and appropriately at your back when he escorts you across the street. He will not laugh at jokes that demean women. He may not necessarily be a Hollywood-handsome man, nor perhaps as fit as a fiddle, but he is well-groomed and marvelously well-mannered. He will kiss your hand to say, "Hello," when he gets to know you. He is always polite. If you are dating, he will bring flowers, may prepare a meal with candles, or send you a sweet thank you note after a date. If holding the umbrella over your head rather than his own means getting wet, he gets wet. Although well-groomed, he willingly gets dirty if it means helping a woman change a tire or carrying a child who has soiled his/her clothes. He has a nice stride in his walk, but he does not act cocky or in a conceited manner.

**Contemplation**: Who would not be charmed by this man who "dotes on you in little sweet ways" and who respects womanhood? Such treatment can be so refreshing! One could feel very feminine and womanly around this man. Who would not want to be around him after a long or arduous day?

**Reality**: Such men may dote on you more than you may want. For example, he may be so chivalrous that he may create dependence in you. You can easily get drawn into his doting, and when you seek a break to perhaps go out with your friends, he may go into helicopter mode. He may want to drive you to and fro, and for you to call periodically for him to know that you are safe. Alternatively, being charming, romantic, and debonair does not automatically mean being responsible, diligent, or emotionally mature. His purposeful chivalry may be compensating for a lack of other valuable and important life skills, such as sound financial management, or setting limits and making consistent contributions to training children. He may expect to be forgiven for such deficiencies in light of his having been the epitome of charm, grace, and chivalry in his personal interactions toward you.

# CHAPTER 6

## ONE WHO TAKES EXCELLENT CARE OF HIS BODY

**Profile**: This man jogs, works out, and eats healthy. He is very fit and looks good. He is a firm believer in taking care of one's body and that living healthy is a good witness for the Lord. He encourages others to do likewise. Perhaps he works full-time but also has a part-time job at a gym, has a garden in his backyard, and his home is filled with books on health. And although he is as fit as a fiddle, he is not conceited; in fact, he hates being in the spotlight.

**Contemplation**: Who would not be desirous of a man who looked good to the eye and maintained a great body? A healthy body is a wonderful asset, especially if he also takes good care of the inside of that body. After all, Christ asks us to respect our body temple wherein the Holy Spirit dwells. This man will be extra appealing, as he does not appear conceited and shuns fanfare about his looks. You respect his passion for healthy living and being an advocate of healthy eating and disciplined care for the body, especially if you do likewise or if you benefit from encouragement in this regard. Were you to become a couple, you imagine doing health seminars or health fairs together. You are tempted to imagine that if he takes such good care of his body, he will take equally good care of you.

**Reality**: Just because he has embraced God's plan for healthy living does not mean he has likewise embraced God's plan for a healthy partnership or marriage. I go back to vulnerability. He may elevate his passion for healthy living to become a wall between himself and building healthy relationships. When the going gets tough, will he stand strong together with you, or will working out become his retreat or escape? His exercise equipment may become your competition. He may feel powerful and in control in the gym, but still act insecure and fearful in a relationship.

# CHAPTER 7

## KNOWN TO HAVE BEEN A GOOD HUSBAND
## TO HIS FORMER WIFE

**Profile**: We sometimes hear about or actually witness the behavior of a widower who was known as a great husband to his former wife. We learn of his loving ways and commitment to her. Perhaps we grieved with him because we could see the devastating loss. You have witnessed many women subsequently try to get his attention, yet his responses appear cordial but uninterested. After more time elapses, eventually you end up working together on a church committee, and he seems to give you more attention than he did all those other women. His interest does not appear phony or contrived, but appropriately engaging and surprisingly pleasant.

**Contemplation**: Wow! You are flattered. You wonder what might be so special about you that he gives you more attention than the others. Intrigued, you continue working with him on the committee; after some time passes, you begin to casually date. You are tempted to wonder if maybe he could love again; you dream about the possibility.

**Reality**: While he may have been a great husband to his former wife, this fact does not automatically translate to his being a good husband to you. We are all different; we all have different chemistry. What he and his late wife had working for them was their chemistry, not yours. We have different strengths and weaknesses; perhaps theirs matched up well, complementing each other. We are also spirit beings, and perhaps something about your spirit reminds him of his late wife and has now drawn him to you. But while you may be the person he has now come to really enjoy being around, it could still be that the special something that he had with his wife will remain only with his wife, and not you. Another important consideration is the uncertainty around how long it takes for his former spouse to become a pleasant memory, and no longer a permanent fixture in his mind.

# CHAPTER 8

## A GREAT ABSENTEE DAD

**Profile**: This divorced man seems to be always with his kids, whose primary residence remains with their mother, the ex-wife. He seems to greatly enjoy their company, and his interaction with them is admirable. People know not to ask him to do things when it is his turn to have his kids because he makes them a priority. He not only does fun things with them but also educational outings. He role models well. He makes sure his children are respectful of others, especially adults. He insists they use good manners. One can sense his disappointment when it is time for him to return the children to their mom.

**Contemplation**: You view him as the best absentee dad that you have ever seen. You and others admire how he behaves with his children, and how steadfast he is about their importance in his life. You may be especially drawn to him if you had the experience of a distant father or if the father of your children has misplaced priorities. He may also relate well with adults, even when he does not have his children. You are tempted to think he possesses a winning combination: both relatable + committed to his children.

**Reality**: This man will likely be pleasant, well-mannered, and respectful of you. He may spend some time with you, but if he will not step up and commit, at least four possible mental roadblocks may be interposing to inhibit a healthy new relationship:

(1) the failure of the first marriage may have created an understandable hesitancy or fear of commitment, and he can always safely use his children as an excuse to not be available, present with, or supportive of you.

(2) He may want to lead two lives, one when with his kids, and another of valuing the total freedom to do whatever he desires (positive not negative things) when not with his kids, which may include you, but not as a priority.

(3) He loves being with his kids, but he may not want to parent anyone else's kids; or

(4) He may not want a stepmother in his children's lives.

# CHAPTER 9

## A GOOD COOK AND HOUSEKEEPER

**Profile**: This man is well-known for his culinary talent, while also having no fear of housework. He espouses that these two chores are not automatically a "woman's job," instead firmly believing in equality in these areas. He typically cheerfully participates in both church potluck preparations and cleanup. He puts on a nice spread when he invites people to his well-maintained home. He finds cooking relaxing and therapeutic.

**Contemplation**: What woman would not welcome having a man who not only performs his share of cooking and housework but does so well, without the need for prompting or coaxing? You conclude that he must be a "modern-day" man because he espouses this equality between the sexes and is not afraid to demonstrate it. You are in awe of this man's gifts and talents, and you are tempted to believe that this sharing attitude speaks to his being a supportive and committed potential mate.

**Reality**: This man will surely cook and clean for you with no hesitation, but his commitment to household duties does not automatically translate to "bonding" with you. Cooking and cleaning are physical actions that can get misinterpreted as: "I am ready for a healthy partnership;" or "I am a 21st-century man who could sync well with a life partner who works a full-time demanding job." Like the man who is charming and debonair, this man may expect you to excuse his inability to bond with you because he is such a great "helpmate" in the kitchen and around the house. Cooking and cleaning may become his escape from dealing with the worrying realities of married life or from working on his relationship with you. So while you might have good meals and a clean house, beware that you could end up being well-fed, yet lonesome.

# CHAPTER 10

## A PASTOR OF A CHURCH AND
## PREACHES GREAT SERMONS

**Profile**: This man of God is admired by parishioners and fellow clergy alike. He is a gifted speaker, and his sermons are substantive, thought-provoking, and salvation-focused. He relates bible stories to real-life experiences. He is an organized church leader and does his pastoral duties well (e.g., visits the sick and shut-in, makes encouraging contacts with members, advocates evangelism, works with his elders to be role models, and conducts board meetings in a fair and orderly fashion). Importantly, he remains level-headed when things get heated.

**Contemplation**: Some women long to have the first lady title. Their reasons may vary:

(1) She honestly feels she would be a good "help meet" for a pastor with all his spiritual responsibilities;

(2) She was a "pastor's kid" and knows firsthand what her dad had to endure;

(3) She loves the thought of being first lady and at her husband's side;

(4) She longs for a man who is genuinely sincere about his relationship with the Lord, never mind that it comes with

pastoring a congregation.

**Reality**: Preaching about and teaching others to live a Christ-like life does not automatically translate into faithfully living out such a life. For example, a pastor may be an extrovert in public, but an introvert at home. He may feel safe connecting with church members because he does not have to live or sleep with them. A pastor may truly be sincere in what he preaches, but that does not mean he can connect on an intimate level with a lifetime partner. Intimacy takes work, commitment, and vulnerability. Also, a pastor who struggles with working on relationship issues may defer to his pastoral duties as a way of escape.

# CHAPTER 11

## TELLING YOU THAT GOD HAS TOLD HIM
## THAT YOU ARE THE ONE FOR HIM

**Profile**: Though this man may not be a pastor, elder, deacon, or church official, yet he is a very spiritual man and has a kind personality to match. Everyone believes his actions display a reverence for God. His prayers sound so powerful that they bring tears to your eyes. He is the "Go To" guy when church members need assistance with a program (e.g., he will fill in if the scheduled person is unavailable, whatever the duty). He readily steps up to the plate if the pastor needs someone to visit the sick. He loves assisting with evangelistic efforts by following up with visitors who request bible studies.

**Contemplation**: Yes, a Christian woman would be drawn to this man. You believe that God must have his hand on this man, who is not only very helpful in the church, but says awesome prayers and has a hunger for souls. After some time of dating, he tells you that "God has spoken to him about you." This declaration quite moves you. You are tempted to accept that since he is so spiritual and prayerful, maybe God really has spoken to him, and therefore "YOU ARE THE ONE!"

**Reality**: It is possible that God could in fact have spoken to this man about you, but you are not directly privy to any dialogue between the Lord and him. Yet another possibility that demands consideration is that the man misheard God, perhaps because you may have qualities to which he is strongly attracted or you fit the imaginary profile that he has created in his mind for the ideal woman. There may be nothing amiss about his thought process, or his attraction to you. He may sincerely believe that because of your better qualities or of your fitting the "profile" that he believes God has set down as ideal that you are to be his life partner. The question that you need to ask and pray about is whether God has clearly revealed the same message to you. If the message of a holy union between you both truly be of God, assuredly God will speak clearly to you as well. Always remember that God does not give mixed messages, and He is not the author of confusion.

# CHAPTER 12

## MEETING 80-90% OF THE MARKS ON YOUR FUTURE MATE CHECKLIST AND VICE VERSA

**Profile**: You have had tangible dreams of the type of man that you want in your life. But your prayer has always been, "God send me the godly man whom you want as my life partner." You understand and accept that whomever God has in mind for you might be very different from the one whom you have been imagining. Then one day the unexpected happens; you meet someone and begin interacting. After many months, when you talk or see each other, you note that he is gaining more and more checks on your list. In turn, he tells you that you are gaining more checkmarks on his list as well.

**Contemplation:** You are baffled and thrilled at the same time. Why? Baffled because you can hardly believe that "dreams do come true." You have often thought that is the stuff of fairy tales. And yet thrilled because you are so enjoying this man who appears as a manifestation of your very dreams. You are strongly tempted to believe that God has finally given or is giving you the desires of your heart.

**Reality**: HOLD UP!! This man could very well have nearly all the desirable checkmarks about which you have dreamed, and you may likewise be the manifestation of what he thinks he wants in a woman. While this sounds like a match at least nearly made in heaven, simply meeting marks on a checklist alone does not represent a "Go" sign from God. Even being on each other's checkbox list does not itself equate to a healthy and happy marriage. Certainly, having a spouse who meets or exceeds our expectations is highly desirable, but are our expectations reasonable and our desires the right ones? Our major checkmarks must be spiritual ones (e.g., How does he see his purpose on earth?; how does he see marriage biblically?; what is his view on serving each other?; does he understand what being "present" means?; and is he respectful of your individual relationship with God?) Moreover, how crucial are the issues involved in the 10-20% of your list in which he does not check the box?

# CHAPTER 13

## THE CONCLUSION

By now you might be thinking, "Gosh, every potentially prospective partner is discouragingly flawed." Listen, God tells us that we are all flawed!!! To expect otherwise is to not be in touch with reality. If you expect to find the "perfect" man, then you best be content being married to Jesus only---because He is the only truly perfect man.

As such, I pray women do not feel "doomed" when reading this relationship handbook. The writer's goal is not to discourage, but rather to encourage women to step back, take a deep breath, and carefully and prayerfully study the man whom you are contemplating as a life partner or with whom you are spending meaningful time. Strong and delicate emotions are involved in relationships, and we must be careful not to allow the enemy to deceive us, or to be self-deceived. We need to accept God's warning counsel that our hearts are deceitful above all things and desperately wicked; thus, when it comes to so important and life-altering a decision as the choice of a spouse, we need to trust ourselves and our feelings less, and less, and trust all to God's gentle leading and loving care. Our feelings are not unimportant, but just not a reliable guide; when it comes to issues of the heart, the principle must reign over feelings alone. Toward this desired end, please consider the following suggestions:

1. Nurture your relationship with God daily through bible study, prayer, and a practical living witness, so that you can clearly hear His voice guiding your every life decision, especially about a permanent relationship.

2. Petition God to direct the Holy Spirit to remove you from any relationship that interferes with a healthy spiritual relationship with God first, or that will separate between you and God, or between him and God.

3. Know what the bible says about respectful relationships; read-only biblically based spiritual books on intimate relationships.

4. Seek a born-again accountability partner, pastoral counseling, and a faithful prayer group to help you stay spiritually grounded.

5. Refrain from sexual intimacy outside of marriage, which will not only cloud your judgment, but will also open unwanted avenues of mental anguish, such as shame, guilt, anxiety, and despair.

6. Maintain a vibrant life independent of your potential partner, so that you are not "solo" focused on the relationship;

volunteer, workout, take up a new hobby, do ministry, travel, etc.; and

7. Ask God to mold you to be the person that He wants you to be at all times, whether for singlehood now, or for a future life and blessed calling that He has planned for you with your future mate!

# ABOUT THE AUTHOR

L inda Sheridan loves God and Jesus Christ whom He has sent. The author herself has, over the years, either contemplated one or more of these profiles or has talked to many other women who have done likewise. As such, she views this work as a "sister-to-sister" book of loving concern and joyous hope. She simply wants Christian women who truly appreciate that "one" special asset in a man that they find most appealing, yet not allow it to become the determining factor of their final decision in his becoming her life partner. She rather prays that the determining factor in every decision of life (and especially those most important to our heart and eternal salvation) be to please their friend God and bring Him glory!

# BIBLIOGRAPHY

**Title**: As For Me and My House: Crafting Your Marriage to Last

**Publisher**: Thomas Nelson Publishing, 1990 Expanded Edition


**Title**: Lies At the Altar: The Truth About Great Marriages

**Publisher**: Hyperion Publishing, 2006


**Title**: Scared Marriage: What If God Designed Marriage to Make Us Holy More Than To Make Us Happy?

**Publisher**: Zandervan Publishing, 2000 Edition


**Title**: The First Two Years of Marriage

**Publisher**: Paulist Publishing, 1983

www.ingramcontent.com/pod-product-compliance
Lightning Source LLC
Chambersburg PA
CBHW051249120626
46547CB00014B/1868